W9-BED-698

Science to the Rescue

Trapped on the Rock

Can science save your life?

Gerry Bailey

Crabtree Publishing Company
www.crabtreebooks.com

Crabtree Publishing Company
www.crabtreebooks.com
1-800-387-7650

PMB 59051, 350 Fifth Ave.
59th Floor,
New York, NY 10118

616 Welland Ave.
St. Catharines, ON
L2M 5V6

Published by Crabtree Publishing in 2014

Author: Gerry Bailey
Illustrator: Leighton Noyes
Editor: Shirley Duke
Proofreaders: Kathy Middleton, Crystal Sikkens
Production coordinator and
 Prepress technician: Tammy McGarr
Print coordinator: Margaret Amy Salter

Photographs:
All images are Shutterstock.com unless otherwise stated.
Cover – Ttphoto Inserts (t) SIHASAKPRACHUM (m)
Vadim Petrakar (b) Matyas Arvai
Pg 1 - Corepics VOFi   Pg 2/3 - Det-anan
Pg 6/7 – SIHASAKPRACHUM Pg 7 - Andrea Danti
Pg 8 – (t) daulon (b) daulon   Pg 9 – (tr) daulon
(tl) robert cicchetti (br) alltoz696
Pg 10/11 - kojihirano Pg 13 – (tr) Chantal de Bruijne br)
Alberto Tirado (bl) falk Pg 14 /15 Tom Bean / Corbis
Pg 15 - (t) iBird (b) huebi71 Pg 16/17 – Dennis Donohue
Pg 17 – (m) Bridget Calip (r) Robert Kelsey (l) Christopher Kolaczan Pg 18/19 - Michele Alfieri
Pg 19 – (t) Micha Klootwijk (b) Dumitrescu Ciprian-Florin
Pg 20/21 – Dainis Derics Pg 20 - S. Kuelcue
Pg 21 – chalabala Pg 22/23 - Mboe
Pg 23 – Glenn Kershner Pg 24 – (t) Roberto Romanin (m)
James Martin Phelps (b) hajes
Pg 25 – (t) Vitalfoto (m) Matyas Arvai
(b) kurdistan Pg 27 – (t) Zzvet (m) Blazej Lyjak
(b) Hung Chung Chih Pg 28 – Rich Koele
Pg 29 – (tr) Duard van der Westhuizen
(bl) Mirka Moksha
Frieze – Denis Barbulat

Printed in Canada/032014/BF20140212

Library and Archives Canada Cataloguing in Publication

Bailey, Gerry, author
    Trapped on the rock / Gerry Bailey.

(Science to the rescue)
Includes index.
Issued in print and electronic formats.
ISBN 978-0-7787-0433-1 (bound).--ISBN 978-0-7787-0439-3 (pbk.).--
ISBN 978-1-4271-7545-8 (html).--ISBN 978-1-4271-7551-9 (pdf)

    1. Mountains--Juvenile literature. I. Title.

GB512.B35 2014   j551.43'2   C2014-900928-3
                                           C2014-900929-1

Library of Congress Cataloging-in-Publication Data

CIP available at Library of Congress

Contents

Joe's story

Hi! My name is Joe, and I've just returned from another adventure. This time it happened in the mountains—high up on the craggy slopes.

I was making my way over the rocks when there was a tremor. I'll tell you all about tremors later, but as I was standing there, the ground under my feet gave way. Down and down I went, until my guide rope tightened and I was hanging in the air.

Well, I managed to get myself onto a ledge. Thanks to some great guides, animals, and people, along with all the science I know, I finally got back down to the valley.

So, let me tell you all about it.

I had been climbing all day and I was tired. My climbing equipment was feeling heavier and heavier, and the ground was growing steeper and steeper. As you climb higher, there is less and less oxygen in the air. Now, we humans need oxygen to breathe, so I was also getting out of breath.

I knew I had to be high up to find what I was looking for. The area of rocks I wanted to look at were clearly marked on the map. I just had to get there.

What is a mountain?

Mountains are areas of land that are much higher than the land around. Groups of mountains together are called mountain ranges or chains.

Tectonic plates

Earth's **crust** is made up of a jigsaw of enormous sheets of rock called tectonic plates. About 12 large plates and 20 smaller ones make up this jigsaw.

We map a mountain using circular lines called contour marks. Each line shows a different height level.

The plates are constantly moving and often collide or slide past each other. The heavier oceanic plate will dive underneath the plate moving toward it, and the lighter continental plate will be pushed upward to form a mountain chain.

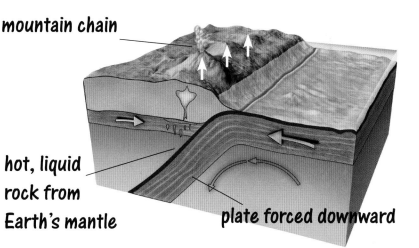

mountain chain

hot, liquid rock from Earth's mantle

plate forced downward

Mount Everest is the highest mountain in the Himalayas, a mountain chain formed by the collision of tectonic plates.

I had been squeezing myself into cracks and crevices all morning. The mountains had been stretched and creased into rough, rugged shapes over millions of years. There were many holes and narrow spaces where the rock had been broken and shattered to pieces.

Different shapes

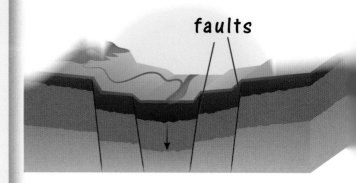

faults

Block mountains

Sometimes tectonic plates move, causing Earth's crust to stretch and split into blocks. Cracks called **faults** appear between the blocks.

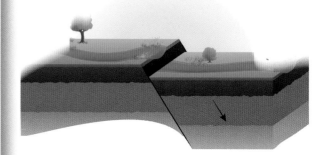

Some blocks may sink to make steep-sided valleys. The blocks that remain high on either side are called **block mountains**.

Fold mountains

Fold mountains are folded into shape as tectonic plates collide or slide over each other, forcing the land to crumble and wrinkle under the pressure.

Layers of rock that have been folded by tectonic forces can form mountain ranges.

lava

magma

Volcanic mountains

Volcanic mountains are cone-shaped and formed by hot, molten rock called magma. Pressure forces magma out of an opening, where it creates a cone shape as the liquid rock, now called lava, leaves the volcano, cools, and hardens.

Plateau mountains

Plateau mountains are formed by large regions of flat land uplifted by tectonic forces or layers of lava flows that build up. A few plateaus form when rivers carve away the sides, leaving the high, flat rock.

Layers in the rock

When you look at the side of a mountain that's been worn away, you often see layers of different materials or colors. These layers are called strata. They exist because different types of **sediment** have been laid down over time and changed into rock. The further you go down into Earth's crust, the older the rocks are.

What are the strata made of?

Animal skeletons mixed with chemicals from sea water become **limestone**.

Mud becomes shale.

Sand becomes sandstone.

Hard granite from lava lies underneath.

Strata are usually made of sediment that has been deposited on the floor of the sea. Sediment might be made of mud from a river, sand from beaches, or parts of plants and animals that have died. Over millions of years, more and more layers build up, pressing down on the older ones. The pressure turns the soft sediment into rock.

Erosion

Erosion describes the process where broken pieces and bits of rock are moved away from their source by water, wind, and ice. Weathering causes rocks to break apart and then erosion moves them. Mountain erosion leaves jagged peaks and deep valleys that smooth down over time by further erosion.

Erosion by water, wind, and the Colorado River has revealed the rock strata of the Grand Canyon in Arizona.

I was up in the mountains to do some **paleontology**. That's a long word to describe the work of someone who looks for ancient remains and **fossils** in the rocks.

As the different layers of rock settled over hundreds of thousands of years, the remains of dead plants and animals became trapped in the layers. The deeper you dig, the older the remains will be.

I had brought my tools with me: a rock hammer, magnifying lens, a soft brush, chisels, tweezers, and a flat-bladed palette knife, which looks much like a putty knife.

The fossils have to be very carefully removed from the rocks, and then cleaned and studied back in the laboratory. I was soon filling my bag with samples to take back with me.

Fossils on the mountain

A fossil is the remains of a plant or animal that lived long ago and has been preserved in rock. It can be an entire skeleton, a single bone, a leaf, or a set of footprints.

Fossils show us what kinds of plants and animals lived hundreds of millions of years ago. They help scientists date rocks, as well as understand the kind of world that used to exist.

These fossils are of trilobites which are extinct marine animals.

A prehistoric fish fossil

These insect fossils were trapped in amber, the sticky substance given off by trees.

Usually animal fossils occur when an animal dies in muddy sediment near or under water. When it decays, it leaves a space in the surrounding ground. This is a mold. Over time, the mold fills with minerals that harden into a fossil.

But just as I spied the first fossils in the rock face above me, the ground started to shake.

It shook the stones beneath my feet and I lost my balance. Fortunately, I was harnessed in and roped to the cliff, but it was a dangerous moment.

Crumple and crack

As mountains are formed, the rocks are put under great pressure. They may start to crack and shift, and this movement causes shock waves, or tremors, through the earth. This is known as an **earthquake.**

The earthquake's size is the amount it shakes. The motion is measured on the Mercalli scale. A gentle tremor is point 1. The strongest is point 12. The spot underground where the earthquake takes place is called the focus. Directly above, on the surface, is the **epicenter,** where the greatest tremors are felt.

The San Andreas Fault in California is shaken by frequent earthquakes.

A strong earthquake will demolish homes.

A machine called a **seismograph** measures the shaking of an earthquake.

earthquake

I couldn't dangle there forever. Using all my strength, I hauled myself up the rope to the ledge above.

From there, I looked around to see what was around me. I wasn't alone!

Mountain animals

A mountain lion, also known as a cougar, is a big cat. It often feeds on deer and small animals at night.

A pika is a small brown mammal with large, rounded ears. It makes a den in rock piles that collect at the foot of the mountain.

Grizzly bears dig dens in the sides of hills or mountains where they hibernate for the winter.

Elk are one of the largest species of deer. They are found high in mountains in early spring.

Mountain regions become very cold in winter and at night. They can also be quite windy.

Mammals that live in the mountains need thick fur and wide feet that won't sink into snow. Some mammals, such as certain ground squirrels, hibernate during winter months.

In the cave

Caves are rock hollowed out by water that has picked up a gas called carbon dioxide. This gas has been released by rotting plants in the soil, and it turns the water into a weak acid. When the acid water passes through cracks in rock, such as limestone, the rock dissolves.

Dripped shapes

As the water and dissolved limestone drip throughout the cave, the carbon dioxide gas evaporates. This leaves a mineral called **calcium carbonate**, which hardens into pointed shapes as it drips to the cave floor.

The cracks get bigger and bigger until a cave is formed.

The roof structures are called stalactites while the floor deposits are called stalagmites.

Fly like an eagle

An eagle is a large **bird of prey**. There are 60 different species of eagles living around the world. The eagle has a hooked bill and powerful curved claws, or talons, to help it grip and tear meat. It relies on sharp eyesight to spot food, even from high up in the sky.

Eagles have a large wingspan, which is the measurement from the tip of one outstretched wing across to the tip of the other. The shape of their wings helps them glide and fly.

An eagle's eyesight and hooked bill helps it catch and eat small animals such as rabbits, snakes, and fish.

20

How do birds fly?

A bird's wing is shaped so that air rushing over the top of the wing speeds up. This decreases the **air pressure** above the wing. Air pressure is the weight of air. Air speed and pressure below the wing remain normal. As the bird flies, the air pressure is higher under the wing and pushes upward. This force is called lift. Lift helps a bird or aircraft fly.

The wings of an airplane are shaped like a bird's wings.

21

I enjoyed watching all the birds and animals of the mountains. But this is where they belonged—and I didn't. I wanted to get back down the mountain. But how? I could hear a waterfall thundering over the cliff. Was that the only way down?

Luckily for me, help came from an unexpected place...

Downhill flow

Water always moves downhill. This is because it is being pulled downward by Earth's force of **gravity**. The steeper the journey, the faster the water flows.

Waterfalls crash down onto the ground below, wearing it away. They also wear away the rock they're falling over.

Gravity

Gravity is a force that pulls things toward each other. The strength of the pull depends on how far apart the objects are and how much **mass**, or matter, each one contains. The greater the mass, the greater the force of gravity an object will have.

Both Earth and people have a gravitational pull. Earth is much larger, so its pull on us is greater than our pull on it. That's why we stay on the ground.

Fast-moving rivers are great for kayaking.

The hoof of a mountain goat is split into two toes that spread wide to improve balance.

Right at my side, perched on a narrow ledge—a lot like the one I was clinging to—was a mountain goat.

Mountain goats can jump nearly 12 feet (3.6 m) in a single bound.

"Come on," it seemed to say. "What are you waiting for? Are you afraid of heights?"

"Are you coming or not?" another seemed to ask. "All you need to do is follow us!"

They made it look so easy! Over the years, they had worn a narrow path down the mountain. It was familiar ground for them.

But not for me!

I tried to tell them I didn't have the special hooves that allowed them to grip rough rocks or ice. Their hooves have a hard rim with a soft, spongy pad inside.

Herds can include as many as 20 goats.

Still, I wasn't going to show them how terrified I was. So, plucking up my courage, I set off, step by careful step, behind them.

And they brought me safely down.

As I came down the mountain, I saw a group of guides. They had been sent to look for me and help carry my fossil samples back to our base camp.

After my adventure high up on the mountain, I promised that next time I would take them with me.

Mountain people

It's not just animals that live high in the mountains. People live there, too.

The Sherpa people live in Nepal, in the Himalaya mountains of Asia. They are expert mountaineers with knowledge of the landscape. They often work as guides on climbing expeditions.

A Sherpa guide

Sherpas act as porters carrying heavy packs.

In 1953, Sir Edmund Hillary and his Sherpa guide, Tenzing Norgay, became the first people known to have reached the summit of Mount Everest, the tallest mountain in the world at 29,000 feet (8,848 m).

Mount Everest

Sherpas, like other mountain peoples, have developed bodies adapted to living at high **altitude**. The higher you climb, the less oxygen there is in the air.

Mountain dwellers have more hemoglobin, the part of the blood that carries oxygen, and their red blood cells are larger. Thicker blood means they have a bigger, stronger heart to pump it around—sometimes around one-fifth larger than normal. Their lungs are larger, too.

A statue of Tenzing Norgay

Of course, my day on the mountain was exciting, but back in the lab, well, that's when the real excitement starts. Maybe we discovered some completely unknown plant or animal that lived millions of years ago!

So here we are, where we came in. And as you can see, I'll be busy for some time...

Why is Joe there?

The study of fossils is known as paleontology. Joe is in the mountains working as a paleontologist.

Once he finds fossils, he returns to the lab with them to study them. A lot of information about the lives of extinct animals and plants can be learned by studying fossils.

A paleontologist uses tools such as picks and hammers to chip away rock, sieves to sift through dirt, and brushes to dust off artifacts.

Carbon dating

Carbon dating is one method used to find out the age of bones and fossils. It measures **radioactivity**—the way certain substances such as rocks and gases give off a form of the **element** carbon. Carbon breaks down so slowly most objects have some remaining for long periods of time. The amount of carbon left in a fossil helps scientists calculate the fossil's approximate age.

Fossils are labeled and stored on site. This is important because bones may be rebuilt to form an animal's skeleton later.

The ammonite was an early shellfish. It could grow to be more than three feet (1 m) long.

Index fossils are fossils that are always found in rock from a particular time. This makes it easier to date the rock and the fossils in it.

Glossary

air pressure
A measurement of the weight of air pressing down on the surface of Earth

altitude
Describes the height of land above sea level

bird of prey
A bird that eats meat and hunts animals for food

block mountains
Mountains that form when there is a split in a tectonic plate, causing sections of land to slip and form a lower valley or uplift above the surrounding land

calcium carbonate
A calcium salt that is made from carbon, oxygen, and calcium. Calcium carbonate is the main part of the limestone rock

crust
The hard outer surface of a planet such as Earth

earthquake
A large, sudden movement of Earth's surface, or its crust

element
A substance made of the same kind of atoms, like carbon, hydrogen, and oxygen, and that combine to form all matter

epicenter
The point on Earth's surface directly above the center of an earthquake

erosion
The moving of rocks and soil caused by weathering. Water, wind, and ice carry away the weathered material

faults
Cracks in the rock caused by movement in Earth's crust

fossils
The remains of plants or animals that lived on Earth in a much earlier period of the planet's history

gravity
The force that pulls objects toward one another

limestone
A rock formed from layers of sediment that have been pressed down over time

mass
The amount of matter in something. Everything is made up of matter, which is the material it is made of.

paleontology
The study of prehistoric life through fossils and the rocks that contain them

radioactivity
Energized particles given off by the nucleus of certain elements that is found in specific minerals containing radioactive elements

sediment
A mix of small stones and mud that collects at the bottom of rivers, streams, and on the seabed

seismograph
An instrument that measures how much the ground shakes or vibrates during an earthquake

Learn More...

Books:

National Geographic Kids Everything Volcanoes and Earthquakes: Earthshaking photos, facts, and fun!
by Kathy Furgang.
National Geographic Children's Books, 2013

The Himalayas (Mountains Around the World)
by Molly Aloian.
Crabtree Publishing, 2012

Hillary and Norgay: To the Top of Mount Everest
by Heather Whipple.
Crabtree Publishing, 2007

Websites:

For information on earthquakes in North America:
http://earthquake.usgs.gov/earthquakes/world/?region United%20States

Facts about Mount Everest, the highest mountain in the world:
http://www.sciencekids.co.nz/sciencefacts/earth/mounteverest.html

Index